track is a
Lonely
sport

-nkj

For everyone who read these before they were printed

Contents

A Brief Interlude for Love

A Longer Interlude for Love

the types of poems you'll find here
Thought,
Desire,
Lies, and
Love.

track is a lonely sport
I mean to rest,
I really do,
But still,
I find myself running.

Sit for a minute and
        think, I say.
Sit for a minute and-

Sit for who?
For you, or for me?
It was you, after all, who told me to slow down.

Maybe I will stop.
Just to see if you'll catch up.

No, you've already past me.
You never could take your own advice.
You haven't stopped running,
        Either.

private tickets
Your body
Proclaims a
Gospel of Life, the
Way it moves when
You dance. All of the best parts,
They are there, for the
World to see. But I feel
like I am the only one
Watching.

once
Oh,
I see you.
That is what
you want,
To be Seen.
I approach. That is
what you want,
For me to
approach.
I show interest,
That is what you want,
For me to show.

And I do.
And you hope that maybe there will be more
To this than you expect.
But you know that If
that were the case,
you
Wouldn't still be talking to me.

I know this, too.
That is why I speak to you like I do,
Seem as interested as I do.
It is the only way to get what I want.

Maybe I walk
away tonight,
Continue later.
Or maybe we finish this
Little ritual now.
Either way, we Fuck.

You are left with a hope
That maybe you were
special To me.
I am left with some pictures and a
name, Trophies to show my
friends.

You wish, I wish
How you wish
I cared more than I do.
How I
wish I
could.
Maybe I would,

If doing so
Didn't mean that
I would be pushed

Further

From

You.

Infinity, my Muse
The
Countless
Beautiful
Creations that such slight
Variance in
Order of
Words may
Bring into
Existence
Gives me
Hope that
Anything is
Possible.

From 26
letters,
Endless
Songs.

a birthday
Its my
birthday.
I've never been
a fan of it. An
Entire day for
me. Seems a bit
Pretentious.
Besides,
I've yet to get what I've really
Wanted-

Love.

meow
I admire the way my
Cat lazes by the
Warm fire,
Plump body stretched over the stone mantle,
Soft hair comforted by the
Flame. If only
I could be that
C
      a
  r
         e
      f
            r
        e
e

don't expect a conversation
Sending you a
Message just
so I can
ignore your
response.

a cigar
The
Bitter pull, the
Sharp smoke, the
Flaky paper on your lips, and the
Overpowering
scent of
Dried Tobacco.

I make
It sound like
Hell, but it is
Exactly the kind of
Experience that
Plays into my
Romanticized interpretation of
Manhood.

orbit

I stay away
    from
    You, see

                You once every other week, if that.

                         All
                 We do is

Fuck. I don't give
    You time for

               More than that. If I did,

I might find myself

            Listening to
       Your voice too much,

Hearing the

          Soft words that
              Spell out your Desire,

   Seeing your

           Lips form those
    Lilting notes. I might

                 Fall for
      You.

Right now, you think that

         I am the
            One

   You are
   Orbiting around. No,

        I am
     Orbiting around
       You. If I let
       You
     Tell me everything
          Beautiful about

You,   I would come
        Crashing down and be just
     another
      Use:ass
        Wre\ck ou
   Your pl#anet, a
     Wea/k m'e,ss that
    You d*o n|\ot w@nt but
    wi// She|ter out of
Y0uR   Kind)(ness, a"nyway__s

temperance necessitating a lie
There is
Nothing I
Want more
than to
Throw all
of me at
You. I
Want to be *bound* to
Your
Soul.

But I
Temper the
Attention I give with the
Careful hand of
Patience, so
that I do not
make my
time, the only
offering I
have,
Worthless in
its
Abundance. My

Spirit
Grows fonder of
Yours every
Minute, so I
act as if there
is less
Uniting
us than
Before.

Waiting
I see your
Message
Amongst the 25 other ones.
Yours is the
Only one
I care to open.

I don't.

Instead, I
Wait.

I just stare at it.

It's a
Power
Thing.

me/You

You'll see this
Dynamic as
You read. More accurately, it's
You/me.

an inversion

Just think:
If we acted on every one of our whims,
Where exactly would we be?

Somethings would be better,
Some would be worse.

A lot less people would be virgins.

A lot less people would be alive.

So, in
Other
words:
The dying people would
Live and the living would
Die.

Yours
Legs.
We all have them. I
just like yours better
than mine.

A Ditch

Driving down the
Same road that I have
Countless days
Before, I remember the
One time that it was
Different; I was so
Miserable and
Lonely,
seconds away
from
Swerving into
the Ditch.

Some days,
I'm glad I didn't.

Even though it's only
Some days, those days are
More than enough.

tag

The pen is mightier than the
Sword.
So why is it
That the warriors are the ones sleeping with the
Women?

And the poets are the ones who won't let the
Women
Touch them?

an excuse
I use the slightest
Baseness in
You as an excuse to
Retreat.

Really, the problem is that I
Know you won't ever
Love me until I stop forgetting to
show You why it is I
Love myself.

sealed lips I
want
Her so badly. I
Desire nothing more than to be with
Her
Now. But,
How can I tell
Her that I
Love
Her when my
Silence is the only thing making
Her want me?

a solid 11

Always go for 10's, he tells
Me. But remember,
You're an 11- you're only
dating Down to be Nice.

Strange advice,
But it makes more
Sense than most other things
I have been told. After all,
If you believe you are
Better than
Everyone, they
Might, too, and then
They want nothing more
Than your approval. At that
point, you can
Do with
Them as you please.

possession
To have sex
Sounds too much like
To have coffee.

I was an accident
Remember me? I remember you. I Wanted you.

But you didn't want me. my
Passion was an accident of
Nature, as was I.

Now, I am an Event

I am going to happen to the world,
Much like a storm;
I will not be stopped, and
The world does not get to decide when I arrive
Or when I go. I will be the
Event. Lightning crackling within,
From one end to the other,
Thunder bellowing, all of this
Inside a limited
Domain, yes, but with such
Strength as to impact the EARTH as a whole.
I will *SWEEP* over the dry plains with a
VORACIOUS
FURY and make them
FLUSH with water.
I will start a
FIRE in the Savannah,
And dislodge an
AVALANCHE in the Mountains.
Now, I am an
EVENT.
I do not care about the base things- No.
I am just going to

LIVE.

jealousy
Stop shaming and hating the
Guy who is always
Making out with some girl, like there's something
Wrong with it. you

Know that you would be
Doing it
Too, if-

-if
you could.

I'm too weary
I was in
3rd grade,
Reading under a
Table in the corner of my
Teacher's classroom. The
Story and
Seclusion took me
Away from not
Understanding the
Others. Now, I
Rest in this
Memory.

the sun also rises
Hemingway had it right.
The Sun Does Rise.
Unfortunately,
Jake's cock wouldn't.

a little confused
What does it mean to
be a
Man?
To fuck every girl
Who looks your way?
To love one person so deeply, that the rest become
worthless? Or maybe to be above the
game entirely?

Hell if I know.

maybe these words are me slapping you back; if so, I guess I'm weak, too
I was slapped today. Not by a
Girl, as you'd think. No, it
was a guy.

Well, as much of a guy as
you can be when you need
to slap a dude for talking to
your
Girl.

poetic
What's true
Love? It's the consummation of
Life, it's two people
Lighting the faint
Spark before it
Burns out
Completely.

At least that's what I tell
Them when I want to
Fuck.

you did it for you
you bring us
All doughnuts. nice thing of
you to do. But then
you don't stop asking how they Are, if
We like them.
you didn't do it to be
Nice,
you did to hear us say
yes.

noise on an airplane
The
Child behind me is

Jus -
T

Fig -
Ur -
Ing

Out

Her

Wor -
Ds

Like
That. The
Window shade is
Up. I can
See a
Mountai
n. She
can, Too.

Thaaaaa -
T

Isssss

Aaaaaa

Moun -
Tain!

The
Mother is
trying to
Quiet her.
I welcome the
Noise. It reminds
me of when everything
was
New and
Beautiful.

self-reliance
I'm always going to
Win in the
End, because I have the
Best
Ally:

me.

action moves the clock
I was afraid that I was
Going to
Run out of
Time to
Experience the
Passions of
Youth.

Then, I read a quote in a
Fitzgerald book. His character
Says that he doesn't
Want his
Innocence back, he just
Wants the
Pleasure of
Losing it all over again.

Inaction does not
Move the clock. You actually have to Do
Something to
Bring the
Spring of
your
Years to an
End.

Or,
You could
Die first and just
Lose
It
All, anyways.

Still,
He
Gave me
Hope that I had
Time.

it's intentional

You say that
I make
You feel inadequate.

I Know that's why
You like me.

I Think that
you know it, too.

friends
So hard to
Obtain.
Harder to maintain.
I don't get
People.

So I
Drink of the
Night Sky. The
Stars and the
Moon
Comfort my
Restless
Mind and
Caress my
Soul. They give me a
Sobering
Breath of
Reality.

Life is
Cold. So are the
Heavens. But they are always
Stoic about it.
I am
Not. My
Friends
Teach me how to
Be.

another sonnet

I wonder if Byron wrote under the Moon,
If Shelley asked the stars to check his prose?
Did Keates pray for the night to give him a boon,
And did Kipling look at a star lit rose?
I want to be great, to dance with the Gods
And to drink the nectar of immortality.
I want to wield a pen like a lightning rod
And to write a verse that transcends reality.
Instead of the gods, my company is found in Hell,
I am tormented by countless demons
And mocked by those who I thought I knew well.
Their unbearable proximity stifles my freedom.
I thought with them I should stand,
But now, I ponder: what is it to be a good man?

inconsistency
Some
Girls are hated and ridiculed by
boys because those
boys can't get what they
Want from the
Girls.

Some
girls are Hated and Ridiculed by
boys because those
boys know that the
girls are
Fucking
Annoying.

please stay
Your body speaks to the
Royalty of old, the
Ancient beauty held as the
Highest value of the aristocracy;
Your
Unparalleled aesthetic.

Your curves:
Voluptuous.
Your face:
It holds eyes that know and see all.
Even your feet are:
Divine.

The world, this
earth is far too base for
You to walk on.

I want every part of You,
More than just this once.
My being desires to call You
Majesty, to allow You to have
Sovereignty over myself, to
Own me.

So, after we are finished,
I say the only thing that I know
Will make
You want to
See me another night:

I've had
Better.

Mourning Star

"Lucifer" translates to
Morning Star. With all he had to
Sacrifice to follow
His own
Path, I think that
Mourning is much more
Appropriate.

phantasm

The trees are covered in a thin
Layer of ice.
Each one of their branches, a
Beautiful, sliver of silver
Crystals shining in the morning sunlight.

But, they are only
Now.
Not even today, simply
Now.
They are not an event meant to last, they cannot
Last.
Their beauty is fleeting, already I see them
Melting, dripping from themselves.

The sleeves of ice,
As they warm, they shrink, until
Certain ones become loose enough to
Fall off of the branch, down
To the hard ground below.

I wish you understood this, that
Time is precious. This
Feeling which we can revel in will not be here for long.
Soon, it will
Leave;
Soon, it will
Fall
Under the heat of the warming sun,
Slowly, yes, as if gravity has not fully taken its
Effect. But it will be a
Fall, nonetheless, despite its
Elegance, the beautiful
Crystals that sheath the
Bitter Oak will
Crack and Shatter, their
Shards scattering over the
Hard, Unforgiving
Ground.

a missed chance
The day was not
Seized.
The war that I felt so
Right about winning was
Lost.

I wanted to love,
Voraciously, unhindered by any incarnation of
hesitation. Your mind did not
Allow this. We never even became close enough for me
To mourn what we had.

Instead, I mourn the loss of a
Spark that could have
Lit the most
Vibrant
Flame.

Loading...
I'm trying to
Write. My damned
Document won't
Load. I could use a
Pencil and
Paper. But there could be a
Fire.

Even if I do use a
Computer, I suppose the
World could,
End, we all could
Die, the universe could
Stop, or
Time could
Shatter.

she asked me to write her a poem
It's always the
Ones who want to be
Written about that you can't
find words to describe.

apocalypse
Bukowski saw
Madness at the end,
Byron saw
Darkness at the end.

Lovecraft knew
Madness
always,
Poe knew
Darkness
always.

One man's
Cataclysmic
Upheaval is another man's
reality.

I see
Solitude at the end,
But force
Myself to know it
Always.

deep poetry
Some poetry has to be
Confusing enough to actually be
Deep. It has to Make the
Reader stop and
think: What was that?

It doesn't have to actually
make sense.

another take on armageddon   a   The
Lone boy standing on a   Boy, despite his
Gray pebble beach, a vast,   Few
Endless expanse of   Years,
Stones on   Knows that
Either side of him,   Man will never
Shrouded in Fog.   Imagine it
Perhaps (perhaps used here because it   Again, for man,
doesn't matter) large rocks   man and
Sloping to the sky piled   woman, are
up behind.   Damned to soon
                                                 Cease when

In front, the endless expanse of opaque,
Deep, blue water, stretching out to the   He,
Horizon, with a cooling
Star, a   Takes,
White
Dwarf giving off the last of its   His,
Warmth and
Strange, other   Last,
Worldly
Light before it cools into the largest   Breath,
diamond
Man could ever Imagine.

.

candles
Half burnt
Experiences sitting on my dresser.

cologne
Why
Stand out when you can
Scent out?

the damage done by time

It sounds and
Looks like its
Raining. No, it's
just the
Ice
Falling off of the
Trees in the wind. Only an
Hour ago, I was
Marveling at how fantastic the
Branches looked
Sheathed in their
Glass.
The most
Beautiful things
Are so
Fleeting.

yes, I'm judgmental
I see that
You're not as
Pretty as the
Others.

It just means
You have to
Work harder for
Your spot on
Stage. It
Shouldn't be like
This, but it
Is.

Either
You
Fight for it, or
You get
Forgotten.

So,
You'll
Fight.

Fidelity
She cheated on him.
He knew
It would
Happen.

He had declared it himself over a couple of
drinks:
"Monogamy is
Dead."

Still, there was a
Hope that he was
Wrong.

Her
Infidelity served as
evidence to the
Contrary.

from the perspective of a cynical male

For a
Woman, being
Friends with a
man is a
Power
Thing.

For a
Man, being
Friends with a
woman is a
Sex
Thing.

leverage
Until
You let
him fuck
You,
You have all the
Power.

Unless
he makes you
Believe that you and
your
body are worthless.

Then, the
Power is
his.

a tragedy of 9 months told in 20 short lines
Well,
Who else would
You ask to
Prom, if not
Her,
She questions.

Hesitation from my end of the phone call.

No one, I lie.

In my
Head, I am
Shouting
You, damnit, I
want to ask
You!

I don't
say it, though- I am
on speaker, and her
Boyfriend is with
Her on the other
End.

mutilation

[Spoilers for *The Great Gatsby*]

I am
Nothing like I once
Was. I used to be so
Full of
Love and
Energy and
Life and
Positivity. I
could not Say a
bad word about
Anyone.

Now, I am a
Parody of a younger me,
Twisted and
Lost along the search for
Someone.

That is what the
Quest for love will do to you, it
Will FILL you with
Cynicism and
Anger and
Hate.

If it somehow can't, if
You're just-too-damn-noble, it will fill
You with a
Bullet instead, like
Gatsby.

why do I write about sex?
Why would a 15 year old talk about
Driving?

Forbidden Fruit
I never got to
Taste
Your
Flesh.

That makes
It all the more
Desirable.

not for a show I
want to finally see
you
Dancing for
Yourself.

sorry Why do
you keep
Talking to these other girls? Don't
you really
Like
Her?

I do, I just want some backup
plans, because I'm afraid that
She doesn't like
Me, too.

hope has an inconsistent address
I drive past a
Lane where my
Hope used to
Reside. I didn't realize that it had moved elsewhere until
Now.

future
Move on from the future you
thought you had, or make them
Wish they never
refused to give it to
You in the first place?

a bum
An older fellow,
Glen,
Told me that
Relationships and
making people
Happy are the most
Important parts of
Life.

He saw a
Bum outside on the
Road,
Dressed poorly,
with
Holes in his
Shoes. Glen
Told him to
Come to his
Store the next
Day,
He would give him
Work.

When
Glen got to his
Place in the
Morning, the
Bum was already
Outside on the
Steps. Glen gave
him clothes and a
Job.

Now, the
Bum runs a
Store that does
$4 million in

Sales a year.

He was a
Bum.
Thanks to the
Older
Fellow,
Now
He's
Not.

I'd like to
Imagine
They're both
Happier because of what They could do for
Each
Other.

We'll
leave it there, with a
Smile.

a watch box
So many
Independent
Devices, keeping the
Same
Pace.

                                    Tick-   Tick-   Tick-

Each one so
Different, yet
Crafted for the

                                    Same-   Uniform-   Purpose-

The

                                    Same-   Time-   Held-

by
All.

                                    Tick-   Tick-   Tick-

one constant
I used to be "good."
Now I'm
Not.

People
Change.

But I
Still
Want
You.

That won't
Change.

You and my
Desire- they're
constant.

(But that's two?)

Not Quite a Sonnet

On the horizon,
I view the fire of the setting sun,
A bright red band of many colors,
Burning as one.
Flame is coming from far off the shore,
Over the great vast ocean,
I sense the fast approaching war.
Not one of guns and blades,
But one of fear and loss,
That shall make for me a living Hades.
I know the power of the words
Cannot cause harm to my physical being,
But the mental anguish they can bring about
Almost makes them not worth seeing.

I give this piece these extra 2 to say:
Despite the hurt, I see the words anyways.

a hard decision
She caresses
Me. I let it
Happen. I do
Not reciprocate.
Either I can cuddle with
Her
Now, or
Fuck her again
Later.

Not both. It

Doesn't work
Like that.

an exception
I read part of a
Book every
Night before
I go to
Sleep.
Not
Tonight. No, tonight, I
Try to Read
You.

hoping for hope
The stars are out tonight;
They illuminate the mystic woods with their light.
The summer days are creeping in,
The snow on the ground grows thin.
Still on the war path of desire,
Perhaps the Spring moon will give me a heart on fire.

a form of Irony, but I forgot which one my english teacher said it was
You want to be
Cared for by someone
you Fuck.

I want to be
Fucked by
someone I
Care for.

Instead, you'll
Fuck guys who will never
Care about you,

And I'll
Care about girls who will never
Fuck me.

Looks like it's time
For me to start
Fucking girls who I don't
Care about.

on the back of an Angel
I never go
Bird watching. Except
for the
Time that I did.

I saw a
Little
Brown
One, spread its
Beautiful
Wings, two small arrays of
Feathers,
Glistening black in the
Sunlight.

It's the little things that can make you
Smile.

(and to think that you
thought this one was going
to be about women, too)

(I guess that last bit proves you
right)

ego

There are many solid 6's,
Some 7's, that I could
Easily
Have.

My
Ego, though, won't let
me go below an 8. I don't even consider
Any girl under
That.

I'm certain that is
What makes them
Want
me in the first place.

So, I should just
Stop considering any girl. Problem
Solved.

A Brief Interlude for Love

_____

where are You? (power)
As I lay alone in bed, I know that something is not
Right-
Your
Lips are not
Pressed against
Mine.

too much time away (control)
Tonight,
My
Soul
Yearns for
Yours.

near sighted (assimilation)
Right now, I don't look into the
Future,
Except to
Find the next
Time that I can be
with You.

_____

a rare feminist piece
There is something
Liberating
In the
Sexuality that
Women share together,
The constant kindness and Openness
They allow themselves to experience
that the
men cannot understand.

It is a unity they accept,
A bond forged in
Shared struggles.

2 true opinions and one person just being nice
"Yes, thank
You so
Much,
You did so
Well."

"He's the
Worst."

"Why
does he
think
he's good?"

Either
You let the
Title
Tell you which
Ones are
Important, or
You realize that
None,

Of,

It,

Is,

it's hard to fathom
The underlying
Insecurity that leads me to
Half of my
Decisions

comfort
Everything you've
Told me to make me
feel
better has not
Worked.

Yet, I keep
Asking.

Maybe
I just want to know that
You actually do
Care.

langston hughes

Dreams
Deferred? What about
Dreams
Slashed and
Burned and
Thrashed around in the
Maw of the
Devil,
Voraciously
Ripped to
Shreds before
your very
Eyes?

This is the
greater Tragedy, because the
Remedy is not as simple as saying
Yes to a
Dream; after all, the
dream just said
No to you.

a dried rose
She
Keeps a
Dried
Rose for
Every
lover that didn't last. I
suppose
She has an
Entire fucking
Garden, by now.

What's for Dinner?
I will not
Dine at the table if
Greatness is not on the
Menu.

a scar
She pressed her
Nail against my
Skin- hard. I can still
See the
Scar, and I can still
Feel her
Lips
Against mine.

some more about running
I want to
Bury some things that
Happened in the past.

Running from them
Doesn't work.

Maybe crying about them
Will.

These poems are sort of like
hands digging around in the
Dirt as I'm
Filling the hole with
Tears
Shed over what has
Already happened

And what
Could have
Been.

Still, I keep
Running from the
Grave of the Past, my eyes stuck on it and not
watching what's
Ahead of me.

Soon, I
Run off of the
Cliff.

authentic
couples who
Say that
their significant
other is so
talented and
'"the
best"' give no
Substance. The
Reality of
Compassion is better
Expressed
through the
Medium of
Touch.

what we really need to hear
so you're saying there's a chance? maybe not
now, now we're just friends, but maybe later?

We'll see,
She
responds.

That's her being
Nice. Unless you
Die and are
Reborn as a
Different man,
there's not a fucking
chance.

a broken watch face
I'd like to imagine that you don't
Waste time.
But I'd also like to imagine that I don't
Waste time, either.

Yet here i am.

Not with You.

bested
when you're proving
someone
Wrong,
silence and
action carry the day-
although, I suppose,
silence is an action.

dominance
you're like a dog,
Pissing all over your
territory when you
think someone is
Infringing on it. If you
were truly In charge,
you wouldn't be
Afraid that
I'm going to
Steal your girl.

how to win a damned race

There you are,
With your smug face,
From the finish you're not too far,
But you're going to lose the damned race.
I'm coming from behind,
Getting out of the trap you laid.
There's something you need to keep in mind:
I am one who will not be permanently delayed.
Yes, you can slow me down,
You can interfere with my speed,
But you will not make me frown,
To your words my mind will not heed.
My body you can burn,
Hate towards me you can preach,
All my friends you can turn,
But my thoughts and soul are beyond your reach.
I will not lose.
I will not give up the chase.
Resistance I will choose.
I will *win* the damned race.

trees
Yes, they're
Beautiful, but, from above, they
Block the full
Picture- the
Grand
Image of a
Dynamic
landscape and
Nature is hidden beneath the
innumerable
oaks and pines of my
World.

passion vs love
Love is
Sacrificing for
the sake of
Something you
Care about.
Passion is the
Substance of
Life,
Chasing what your
Soul is
Irresistibly
Pulled to.

Sometimes
they Align.

Sometimes, they
Don't/

You can always
Force yourself to
love. You can't
always
force
Passion to
reignite.

So,
I'll
Always
Pursue

Passion
Over love.

why I never use a treadmill
With all of the
Running from the
Past I've done,
You'd think I'd
Never have to do
cardio again.

making you miss me

When I
Think you
Love me,
I'll stay up,
Talking to
You for hours.

When I'm
Afraid that you
Don't, instead of acting out of
fear,
I'll go to
Sleep,

Making you wait until well into
tomorrow to
Hear my voice again.

impatience
You're somewhat
Interested, but You're
not sure.

I'm somewhat
interested, but I'm not
sure.

The thing is, though, I don't care.

I just want to
Know
You.

eyes and their intent
Other guys at the gym,
I can tell when they
Admire
me. I see their
Eyes darting away, retreating
from my Body when I
Glance towards them. It's
Involuntary. But it
Happens.

When a
Girl
Admires, you and
She
Thinks you might
Admire
Her, too, the
Eyes do the
Opposite. They stay
Locked.

And then, they
Flirt, roll away, as if to
Say: "I'm over
Here. Why aren't
You?"

The future freezes in the air, hinging on your
Response.

expiration date

Love for as long as you

Feel-The-Fiery-Passion.

Once that is
Extinguished, you're
Robbing both
Yourself and
Her of
Someone
Who will
Reignite the
Spark.

L.O.V.E.
Love
Or
Voraciously
Elope

a joke
I saw a
guy wearing a t shirt
that said

'"humble"'

        on it.

you're right, but I'll think you aren't
Yes, I know it's
You, not
Me- after all,
You're the one
whose
Ending
It.

Why, then, does it
Feel like I
could have
done
everything
differently?

I feel like you were lying, but you probably weren't
You tell
me that you
don't want to
Hurt
me, but the
Moment that
Your
Eyes hinted at
Something beyond simple friendship,
I was
Damned to be
Crushed and
Broken in
Your

        nimblehands.

An Ode to the Sea
Sailing under the
Stars, above the
Deep, and among the
Blue waves, with their white caps and
Crashing orchestral percussion, I run my
Fingers along the
Railing, bring them up to my face, and
Licking the
Sea
Salt,
Tasting the
Earth as
She will
One day
Taste my
Corpse, and I allow the
Gentle
Rocking of the
Tide to finally
Lull me into a
Peace.

years
4 years is a long
Time. So is
3 . And
2 . And
1 . A
Single
Day can outlast any of those periods, if
You

Fill it with
Life.

let me know if you see the pattern
He wants
Her. She wants
me. I want
You. You want
Him. He just wants to
Fuck.

it's pretty unfortunate
I still want to be
Loved. But I know that
Whenever I decide to
Open to it, I guarantee
That I will
only
Receive half
of
what I seek.
The other half
will
Stay in
between
Your legs.

a friend that I want too much from
It's
Your
Promising
Grin that
Makes me
Hope,
"Maybe
there will be
More if I
stay by
Your side."

But I know there
Won't
Be. I

Think that
You do,
Too.

I'm hunted, too
Yes, there are
Those who do
Pursue me. But they are
Never the ones who I
Pursue myself.

affirmative action
You don't decide
when Passion
Comes.

So don't let it
Die
Unheeded;

You don't know when
you'll get another
Chance.

choose your own adventure

_____ (insert first and last name of woman you love here),
You are the most
Beautiful Creature to ever have
Existed. In your eyes, I can see the
Cosmos unfold a thousand times over. As I
Run my hand across your silken
Flesh, I *feel* the
Infinite
Constellations in the
Night sky.
Your ass is like the
Moon, each cheek
Round and supple.
When I start at your slender
Feet, the vessels unparalleled in their
Purity, all earned by carrying
You, and work my way up that
Magical line formed where your
Two legs meet,
Perfectly straight, I know that it all, everything I have ever done, is to
Arrive at a
Paradise unparalleled by any of the thousand
Beaches of the gilded tropics. I want nothing more
Than to worship every inch of
You, to
Praise you every way my
Humble being can.

   I
     Love
You.

(and then don't give it to her)

plath
One of
Her
Poems described the doings of a
boy; this Poem is my
attempt to describe the
Doings of a
Girl.

She
Stands
Alone in
Her room. There is a
mirror, but She does
not bother with it.
She begins to
Dance, to
Dance
Alone.

Her little
Ritual of sorts speaks only of
Life, of unbridled
Existence and
Experience.
She is so far
Beyond the
need for
approval.

Afterall,
She
Loves
Herself.

This is what I
wish for Anyone
in a place like
Plath.

Pure,
Unadulterated
Happiness.

throw flour on the ghost

These are feelings that I do
Not understand. So I
Prop them up in
Poems,
Hoping that maybe
then I
Will know Them.
That's
Yet to
Happen. I'm still as
Lost and confused as
When I started. The
Hurt doesn't go
Away. It only becomes
more
Visible.

an outside perspective
'Its not
Nice guys that
Girls like me go
for,' She
explains:

'I was at a concert, and a
Guy walked up to
Me and asked: What's stopping
You from
Fucking me right now?
Nothing, I
Answered.'

subway
I'm sitting on a
Subway. The grown man next to me,
His eyes are
Watering.

He starts
Crying.

His stop is too far
Out. He can't
afford a
Place near the
City.

Money can't buy
Happiness. But it
Helps.

a lesson I want to share
Sometimes,
I wear a very
Expensive
Watch, and compare the amount of
Compliments to the
Times I wear much less
Expensive
watches.

The more
Expensive one gets
Fewer
Compliments than
One that is
Worth 2% of
the
price.

That doesn't
Change the
Value of any of
Them, though.

Make sure that
You
Remember
That.

a paradox
Don't let their
Rejection
Change
You, I'm
Told. But then, they also
Say:
Make them
Regret
Not picking
You. I can't get
over the
Idea that the
Two are mutually exclusive.

the night sky is the most beautiful dress
The little
Stars
Twinkle, like
Bright
Silver
Diamonds, laid out on the
Horizon of a
Deep
Blue
Dress.

a second look

At first glance, I
See no
Stars. I
Turn off my phone, look   *
Again, and
See the   *
Heavens   *   *   *
Lit up.   *   *   *   *   *
          *   *   *   *
                    *   *   *   *   *   *   *
*   *   *   *   *   *
                    *   *   *   *   *   *
                              *   *   *   *   *   *
                                                  *   *
                    *   *   *   *
          *   *   *   *
                              *   *
*   *   *

                                        *

                    *

hold all your questions until the end
As I'm
Making out with
You, feeling each one of
Your perfectly rounded
Curves,
I bring my
Lips to
Your
aquiline
Ear, and
whisper:
I
Love
Yo

ur
bod
y.

compensating for something (someone), no question mark
Running around anywhere
I can, trying to find
Someone else to
Fuck. Sometimes
Successful, sometimes
Not. But every single time that I
Am, I can be
happy for a
minute,
Knowing that I
Accomplished what
You seemed to say that I
Couldn't when
You
Rejected
me.

It doesn't mean
Anything, though-
No matter
How many
Girls I
Kiss and
Women I
Fuck,
I was still
Rejected by
You and- I

still and will
Always
Want
You.

its classy I
wear a
Ring that says:
Conquer.

It's a
Reminder to always
Strive for
Greatness.

Still, I haven't
Gotten
You.

spirits of hellfire

The men who always
Want what they
Can't have, and will do
Anything to get it.

Alexander,
Caesar,
Napoleon.

Men that
Feel they have
So
Much to
Prove, who
Will
Dominate the
Planet for
External
Validation of the
Idea they must
Learn to
Accept themselves,

but never will.

That,
I believe, is what makes them
Great, the
Magma in the
Chest, the
Tormenting torrent of
Flame in the
Mind and Heart that
Says:
No!
You shall not
rest until
Your
labor is done. The
Trials of
Hercules, that

Labor of
Proving that
They are
Worthy of
Love by
Accomplishing more than
anyone else, that
Labor that will
Never be
finished.

Sometimes, I feel like
Them. I am sorry for my
Arrogance, but
Hope that whatever works I
Complete as a
Result of my
Discomfort with Life
will make up for
It.

My
Hope is that being a
Restless, in
Constant
Motion, will lead to
Passionate
Creation and
Discovery in this
Life, and will lead away from
the
Anxiety of not having
Achieved.

Because of
Them, I
Know, deep
Down, how
Wrong I
Am- yet, I do
Nothing to fix it.

ice a
Sculpture made up of an
Ice that melts in the sun of
Inactivity and is
Sustained in the
Cold of
Vehement Motion.

conditional love
I'm going to
Marry a
Beautiful
Woman. She will be a
Stunner. But I will
Resent her. Because
She won't
Sleep with
guys like me until we earn our
Money or we kill
who we once were.

a duality
It makes no sense for me to
Tell you that I
Love and Care
about
You.

So I don't.

It would only make
Things bad, awkward between us- I know that you don't
Feel the same.

But then, what's the point of
Falling for
Someone
if you won't do
Anything because of it?
Be emotional, or
Emotionless. One of the
Two. You can't
Pick one and act like you
picked the
other.

transported I
remember reading
Bukowski outside in the
Summer and
Fall, hearing the birds
Chirping and seeing the sun beams
Illuminate each word
Written by him miles away and decades earlier. Yet, even with the breeze
Cooling me and the chilling water
Quenching my thirst, even with this vivid sensory apprehension of nature,
I was in the
World that He
Wanted me to be-
Alone in a room with cheap booze and cheaper sex.

That is
Art.

stay awake
Get off of me, I tell her, as
she strokes my Body.

She looks
Shocked.

If I let her get too
Comfortable,
We won't
Fuck again.

doing
Again, I wonder what
You are
Doing right now, and ask:
why isn't it me?

a word of advice (about advice)
Don't tell me how to
Do something that I
Know how to do. I will
Look at you and say, thanks for
the advice, I didn't
take it.

not the same
It's different. When
You're
Liked and it doesn't work
Out for the
other, being Friends is still
fun. When
you
like and it doesn't work
Out for
you, being
Friends is hell.

a single second of living
What is it that is so
Special about this
Moment? What
Makes it
Hang
In the air like the
Last note of the
Song that I
Love
So much?
I think it is that
I do not
Want it to
End- I am trying to
Fit fifty years of
Living into one
Instant, so that
I never run out of the
Memory.

blur
I look at the
Clock.
Time has
Passed so
Quickly. The last
Hour has been a
Blur.
Fuck, the last
Week, the last
Month, the last
Year, they all have -

       Like a broad
          Paint
            Stroke,
              You pay so Much
                  Attention to what
                    You're
                  Trying to Create that
                     You
                        Forget to Watch the
                          Stripe of
                            Vibrant
                              Color
                              Appear on the
                              Canvas.

what I'm really looking for I
want a
Deep
Compassion, a
Love that
Transcends
Time. But I am no
Longer
Convinced that its
Real, I've lost
Faith in the
Intersection of
Two
Souls. I don't
Understand how it can be
Reached.

So, instead, I
Write about what
Makes
Sense,
casual
fucking, a
Game in which there are
Rules,
Rules that if you
Follow, you Win.

But all it
Amounts to is a
Passionless
Exchange, two
People
Chasing carnal

Pleasure clothed in a thin
Layer of
Hope,
feeling each other's body so
that they themselves, living
corpses, can
Claw at the top of their dank
Coffins,
Hoping to
Break the rotten wood,
crawl up through the damp
Dirt, and
Catch a
Breath of
Air only faintly less
Insidious than the
Stagnant
Gas built up inside the
Narrow
Tomb that they will
spend eternity in.

Still, it
Makes
More
Sense than Love.

this one has conventional form; it's a sonnet
The ice cakes the branches,
In ah, such a pretty way.
How I wish you were here with me to take chances,
As we near this St. Valentine's Day.
I want to make this year's
One of a love, so untamed,
Free from all base fears,
And left to deeds that are famed.
My heart burst forth with desire,
To see you and see what we can be,
The unholiest lovers I admire,
This passion they, and you, ignite in me.
But you are now sleeping in your bed,
So I fear this love may be confined to just my head.

wistful

Oh, if ever again I could taste of your soft lips,
I would gladly give years of my life to Hell,
If only to once more experience this bliss;
Ah, if so, my soul would be eternally well.
I cannot make it clearer, my friend,
It is you who I voraciously want,
Although it will not be you to the end.
Consistency of desire I promise you not,
But immortality of this vibrant instant,
Endless passion for what is now,
The eternal nature of the fleeting moment,
Is what makes it worth gold in pounds.
Yes, it is going to end one day,
But I want to love you either way.

just Try

Nothing has been perfect for You yet.

It never will be.

But a sad world becomes worse when You stop looking for a happy one.

time
To
Reach
Out and
Pull
Existence straight from the
Air, to
Hold onto
It with the
Strength of the
Bear and the
Resolve of a
Lion, to
Embrace
Reality with such
Fervor that
Time itself
Slows around
You, this is what it is to
Live in the
Now, to
Conquer
Reality when it is most Ripe with
Potential.

Anything
less is a
Complete and
Utter *W*
  A
       S
          T
            E
                  .

chivalry evolves
So much
Time wasted being a
gentleman,
Kissing
hands when I should have been
Kissing
Lips.

passing lane
I sped up in the
Passing lane to get in front of
You just so I could
Slow down to
Exit.

You pull out from
Behind me and
Race ahead. As
You pass, I see the
Fierce
Eyes of a
Woman
Scorned.

I return
Your
Lasers with a
Grin.

Yes, I'm that
Guy that
You
love to
Hate.

separation
Why can't we
Annex off each
Part of
Our
Lives, keep them
Separate, so that the
Emotions of one
Setting don't
Negatively affect the
Emotions of the
Other? Why can't we
Hide the
Sadness of
One
Relationship from the
Participants of another?

I guess if
We could, no
One would truly be a
Part of
Our
Lives at
all.

nice isn't Good
If good things happen to Good
people, then
Every girl and
Every boy who is nice, should be
Happy. Unless
nice
Isn't the same as
Good.

Many times,
I don't think that
it Is.

approval
We all want
It. You think if you
Fuck me you might get
It. Maybe I play into your
Desire.

But only if I
Don't want to
Go again.
No matter what, You
Don't learn to
Love
Yourself.

the self
Unless you
Love you, you'll be
Running around town looking
For someone to do it for you. But
You'll only ask the
People who simply
Never will. Because why would the
love you can come by easily matter to
You at all?

a live pulse
I seek to be a
Man who
Feels the
World's
Heart
Beating in
Tune with his own.

art
If you're not
Inflamed with the
Passion that
Forces you to
Make your
Art, then it won't be a
Living piece. Give it your
Love, your
Hate, your
Pain, your
Joy, your
Joy, your
Suffering, your

Self.

Art only gets the
Life that you give
It. And, as they say,
Art without
Life is

nostradamus

I am Walking in the
Woods and see a deer.
Blood
Spills forth from a
Wound in its chest, directly beneath the
Neck. A
Pool
Gathers below it.

The
Deer
Looks down and
Sees itself
Reflected as a
Wolf in its own
Life fluid. It
Runs in
Fear.

In its haste, it trips on a
Fallen tree, and flies forwards to the
Ground.

The
Wolf walks up to the
corpse,
Sniffs it as if it were
Nothing more than a
log, and then
Saunters
Away.

the tapestry of life has ends

All
Things
Stop.

It is
Painful, beyond
Painful, one of the
Most
Saddening parts of a
Life
Well
Lived.

Days
Spent in
Revelry that
Bleed

                    Far,
                    Far,

into the
Nights,
Passions that
End only when the
Sun
Rises.

I will
Miss them; not just the
Times, but the
Companions that
Made them so
Memorable. These
Hours spent in
Splendor and
Glory will
Live
Forever in my
Heart and
Soul, and
Shall
Never be
Forgotten.

Yes, some
Regrets
Stain

Their otherwise
Perfect Hue.
I'd be
lying if I said that
Everything was
Done as it should have
Been. But to
Live with no
Regrets is to have spent No
Time
Learning.

On the
Whole, the
Vibrancy of that which was
Done will
Forever outweigh the
Shadow of that which was not. If
You can
Achieve the
Balance,
You have
Taken your
Errors and
Missed
Chances and
Grown
Past them, become
More than the sum of
Your faults.

Remember,
You must
Always
Live like
This,
You must always
Live, not in fear, but in
Hope and
Excitement, because
No matter how
Beautiful
They
Are,
                    All
                                        Things

                              Stop

                                    .

similar to Tu Fu's Moonlit Night
Tu Fu asks
When the
Moonlight will
Dry the
Tears he
Sheds for his
Love.

I ask
When the
Moonlight will
Give me
Someone to
shed Tears for.

first kiss
While the
Moment still hangs in the air, while
You can
Feel the
Promise of something
More, of something
Greater, of some
Tangible
Love, while that possibility of
Pursuing
Life exists, it must be
Seized! Don't let the
Tingling on your
Lips, the
Tension in the
Air between the)two
Mouths(, the
Fire and
Electricity
Blazing and
         c   i
   r   n
 A   g
between
Your

Souls

, don't
Ignore it and let it
Die.
Don't let
Life and
Passion slip
Away.

Immortalize this
Fleeting
Connection with the
Physical
Union of
~Your
Lips~

    And before it all or any
        Could be
        Thought,   It
           Occurred.

A Longer Interlude for Love

~1~ Proximity ~1~

the best seat
I love it when
You sit with
Your
Legs
Over
mine.

It makes me
Feel like
You don't
want
me to
Go.

no, it's not
I ask if it is
too
Soon to tell
Her
that I
Love
Her.

She doesn't say anything; the way
She brings
Her
Body closer to mine is the only
Response I need.

free real estate
Nothing is off limits
for
You.
You can touch my body as
You please

But I
Care more about
You
Touching
my soul.

exposed
She
Covers
Her
Chest with
Her hands,
She doesn't want
me to
See
Her so
Exposed.
She is
Unsure of Her
Place here. I ask
Her to show me, anyways.
She does. I am immediately taken away by the sheer magnitude of
Her
Beauty. I
want to
articulate it. I
Cannot. Instead, I
Wrap my arms around
Her and
Hold
Her
Tighter than I
ever have
Before.

my head resting against her chest
The slight
Thumping of
Her
Heart, the
Tempo of
Life kept by a
Goddess.

the best parts of my bed
The
Smell of
Her and the
occasional
Found strand of
once lost Hair.

I'll never understand
How
married
couples
Sleep in the
Same
bed
Every
Night without each other in
Their
Arms.

fire
Time
Burns like a
Voracious
Flame when I'm
not with
You.

hyacinth
I go too Far.
You tell
me to
Stop, in
Your own way. I
Do. Later,
You
Whisper:
"Thank you." I want to
Tell
You that
You have nothing to
Thank me for, what
You have
Given me is
More than enough, that I
wouldn't take anything else
without
Your permission.

Again, I am at a loss for
Words. Instead of sullying the
Moment with impotent noise, I just
Hold
You
Closer.

a pearl in the sand I found
Your earring in
My sheets.
I plan on giving it back to
You, but I
Hope to
Find it
Again, and
Soon.

some positivity
We
Fucked. And now I
Feel her warm
Body against mine. Each of
Us comfortable. Her
Arms, Wrapped around
me, my arms around her.

I let
Her
Heal
me.

~2~ Control ~2~

an Aztec
You
Hold one of my hands in
between the two of Yours.

You
Play with the fingers while
You
Press my palm
Against your
Breast. I
Love
how
You take
me and
put
me by
Your
Heart. I let most
Girls
Play with mine:
You make me
think that I'm
playing with
Yours.

But I
Know that I'm not. Yes, my fingers are
close to
Your
Heart, but
Your fingers are
Wrapped
Around mine.

failed polygamy I
See the sheer
Beauty in other
Girls, too, their
Walk, their
Smile, their
Soul. But all of
that is
Burnt up at an unattended
funeral
Pyre when I'm
Around You.

I'm gone
You pull me
Away on
Tides of
Insatiable
Passion.

I do
Nothing to
Slow
You.

Your
Conquest
is as
Certain as the
Moon's
return above the
Horizon.

a subversive
Our late
Night
Liaisons serve to
Take me away from
my
material
Goals.

It's okay, though, because they're
just *material*, anyways, while our
Meetings
Bring me
Closer
to

        Your
        Soul.

the best compliment
I think that
You might be
Talented,
She says with a
Smirk after
Reading some of my
Poetry. It no longer
Matters to me if
She is
Right; it just
Matters to me that
She
Believes that
She is.

You Win
Temperance,
Patience, and
Caution, all my
virtues, are thrown out by now. It is too
Late for
Resistance.
I have
Completely and
Utterly
Fallen for
You.

For once, I find
Joy in my
Submission.

Power
You
Make
me sorry that I ever
doubted
Love.

Desire
My entire body
Bursts forth with
Desire when I
See even just your
Face;

Your form, when taken on the
Whole, is enough to make me go
Mad. It's fortunate that I was
never
Sane in the first place.

~3~ Assimilation ~3~

An Ode to Life
I love the way that
Life
Expresses itself. A
Baby pulling its
Toes together,
Feeling the
Air. A dog
Trusting a
Man enough to
Expose its stomach to be
Rubbed. A little
Girl
Hugging
Her
Father. A
Cat
Laying in that
Streak of
Sunlight that
Found its way through the
Window. A
Candle
Flickering in a dim room,
Giving off a
Pleasant
Scent and just
Enough
Light. A
Bird
Chirping as I
Look up at the
Ever so
Green
Leaves of a
Tree. The way that
You
Smile.

one star is out
Its
Dark tonight. The
Moon has
Waned into nonexistence, the
Stars
Hide behind the
clouds. Still,
You
Light up my
Soul.

Sweet Reprieve

It's a cruel world,
But how much crueler,
Would it be,
Without you,
Next to me?

the chip off my shoulder
Nothing makes me
Happier than
Knowing that
the
Poems I
wrote about
fucking are
less
True than the
Poems I
Wrote about
Love.

the antidote
Whenever I'm in
Pain,
Anguish, or
Misery, I just
Think about when I
Was with
You, and
All is
Right in the
World.

without you
I can't explain just how
Important
You are to me. I was thinking about
how sad and lonely I was before
You. I don't ever want to go back to
that.

The Value of You
I never thought it was actually
Possible for me to be so
Perfectly in touch and in
Love with anyone as
Beautiful as
You. But being able to
Hold someone who wants to be
Held makes me
Regret how
Wrong I was.

a riddle
Do I
Love
You because I
Love
Life, or do I
Love
Life
because I
Love
You?

other kisses
)She is   ]I am
There(Here[

{We
Change that with
Our
Lips}

why can't I stop?

It's not selfish, I tell
myself.
Selfish would have
been
Keeping
Her and still doing what I'm about to do, anyways.

perception
Focusing on all of the
Missed chances doesn't give
You an
Opportunity to focus on all of the
Beautiful ones that
You did take.

honesty

I'm a
Liar. A lot of what I've written is
Bullshit. I don't fuck all the
Time, contrary to what I make it seem.

Somehow, though, this is
More
True than the
protein shake with spinach I
drink every morning, more
True than the
salad I often have for
lunch.

Those things all
speak To the Great
lie of
self-control, the
False barrier of
"Pride," my
greatest
Vice, but the one that
Holds me back from all the
Other
Foul
Traps.

The stories, though, are about a
World without
Barriers, a place
that is
True because there
is
no filter. The world
Minus
my
pride.

this one is true, I promise
Do
You think we're
Talking?

No.

Well,
you
made
me uncomfortable, I can't
go   to   Prom   with   you
anymore.

What, all I did was
Ask if you would Kiss
me? How is that
bad?

No response.

now, I know that my
only
Crime was being too fucking
awkward.

It doesn't
matter, I can easily
Find another girl to
Walk away from
me.

out

the Quest for Love I
wrote about the quest for
Love turning you

_____ ___.

I said that you get
Lost on the
search for
someone.

I was right, but only if
that
Someone is not
You.

inside

Star Child
Born in a
Supernova, baptized in a
Constellation, and in communion with the
Stars. They say that your
Surroundings help
Make you who
You are. So it's
Wise to
Pick
Good
Ones.

solitude
Alone on the beach, he
looks up at the
Stars.

Nothing
Looks down on him.

infinity
I talk about how the
advent of
increasingly
effective medical
procedures and equipment will let my generation live to at least
150 years of
Age. Maybe I'm
Right. But I
Hedge my
Bets. I still try to
Fit as much
Living as possible into every
Second.

Afterall, I could
Die tomorrow.

sorrow
I hear the shear
Sorrow in
Your
Voice. Nothing is more
Painful to me. The downward
Sloping of
Your
Alto as
You crack and trail off. I think that
Maybe, just
Maybe,
You, too, are
Mourning
              what

Could have been.

the antithesis of all of this
Some of these
poems
Express
Passion, some others
Express a
Disillusionment with
Life. I'm sure that
Hegel would say that this
Paradox puts the
Truth somewhere in the
Middle.

I won't read my daughter fairy tales
The world isn't like a
Fairy tale,
Because the
boys
Never get the
Girl when they're
Prince Charming and the girls
Never get the slipper when they're
Cinderella.

a history lesson
Reading a book about
Ancient
Rome, I think about how
Great it would be to live
There. No time to
Think about being
Existentially

alone

When I'm
trying to
Pacify the
Gauls.

Still, I'm sure I'd find a
Way.

aging A
Good
Kiss makes young lips
Old.

That's what I
once
Thought.

Now, I
Know that the
Inverse is
True. A

Good
Kiss makes
Old lips
Young.

the end
I was told the world was to
End on February the 25th, but I had yet to
Kiss a
Girl. This was a problem, but there were only
Three days left; on the fourth, everything would be
Done.

On the first day, I
Went to school. Perhaps I would
Kiss someone there. Instead, I
learned that Hemingway said:
Never delay
Kissing a pretty
Girl or opening a bottle of whiskey.

So, on the second day, I opened a bottle of
Whiskey. Not to drink, just to
Smell. There was something
Holding me back from tasting as fully as I should.

On the third day, the 25th
Was here. But so was I, my lips still
Innocent. On the third day, I had yet to
Kiss a
Girl. I had no time. So I
Kissed
Myself.

On the fourth day, my
Alarm went off. The world had not, in fact,
Ended. The birds who stayed to
Brave the cold months continued to
Chatter amongst themselves. The trees
Swayed in the wintry wind. And I had yet to
kiss a
girl.

my personal pot of gold
I sit and I
Wonder what is at the end of the
Rainbow?
I hope it is a
Pot of
Gold, I wish
It is. But I'm not actually
Convinced. I think it will be a
Sore back, a
headache,
And regret.

one child only, preferably a Daughter
I want to
Raise a
daughter.
Her heart will be
Broken, but I am sure she will find
Solace in each love she decides to
Pursue, at least
For a time. If she
Really wants to, she can pick a
Boy who will make
Her
Genuinely happy.

I do not want to raise a
Boy. To succeed as he would
Desire to, he'd feel that he would have to become a
Monster. I'd
Love him both too much and
Not strongly enough
To let
That happen.

purity
A child, a
Girl, sets up a table.
She is selling
Cookies,
Flowers, and
Her
Art. I watch how
Happy
She is.

My
Heart
Smiles.

resolution
If you
Expected this to
Wrap itself up, nice and neat and with a
bow on top, then you haven't been paying attention to these
words, or even
Life, for that matter,   .

Ragnarok

In Homage to Byron and Bukowski

The
gods are
Dead. So is our faith in them.
Perhaps lack of the latter
Killed the
Former.

From their
Gargantuan corpses
strewn across the
Waste land,
Hordes of
Doubt
Spill forth over the world,
Heralding in
Conflict like
Battle
priests of old.

The political
Institutions
Fall, just as the
churches did before them.
Our governments crumble,
universities grow
Dull, the
banks erode the value of all
money, and the
alliances are eaten away from
the inside out by Dreaded
Fear.

On the
Sea, ships made of the
Bones of the already
Dead carry the
barely
living towards a
hope shaped like the
Gothic
Castles of the
old
world. When they
Arrive, they find the
wrecks of bricks and
stones and
dreams no better than the
Derelict
Ruins here.

Murder
Barons ride in their
War balloons woven of
human hair and raised by the
Burning of our
Fat and piloted by
Fiends fed off the other
bits of our
Corpses found
scattered across the

land, the last remnants of our
civilizations; they are

Screaming at
whoever has not already
fled to
nowhere,
Spreading
Decrees of
Violence that needn't even be
Cloaked in a thin layer of
"law and order" to be
Accepted.

Those who
Dare
Defy the
End with what little
Strength they have left,
Bolstered by an
Insuppressible
Courage, are
Killed on the
Spot. That
Teaches those who
Thought about
bravery how
False their
Hopes were.

The
Oil wells
Dry up. We
Fight and
Die for them, anyways- it
gives us
Something to
Do.

People
Perish by the tens of
thousands, by the
millions.
Eventually, there are none
left- even the
exploiters of the
masses have
Killed one
another off, but only
After they had
Drained their already
Dying hosts so
Dry that not even
Bones were left to fill the
Mass
Graves, only brief piles of
Dust.

Anything left to remind the
Void of the failed
experiment called
'humanity' is
Scorched in
Hellfire,

Purged, the

Ashes carried far into
Infinity by the
Cold,
Fiercely
Howling Wind
of
Eternity.

The
Horror lands and
once
kingdoms
sink into the
Vast,
Black
Sea of nonbeing, which
Slowly but
Surely
Scabs itself over with the
Ice of
Finality.

The
dead
Gods
Return to a plane that is
Finally
Laden in
Peace,
Quiet, and no sign of their
past
mistake.

To Life
You'll
Have to
Kill
me if you want to
Break me.

just do
That's how
you
end up
Naked on your
roof after
Midnight,
Gazing in
Awe through the
Shroud of
Fog at the
Full
Moon.

walk a little
Maybe
Something
happened that
Stopped
You from reaching a
Goal that
You so
Strongly
Desired, or maybe it's just taking much
Longer than
You had
Thought.

It doesn't matter.

Stop running so much.

No, you must keep
moving,
You don't want to
Spend the only
Life
You have in the state
You will find
Yourself in at the
End:
Stopped.

In Moving,
You've
Lived, and in
Living,
You've
Created.
You'll
Leave here
Knowing that some
Part of some
Life is
Different than it
Was, because of
You, and,
Hopefully,
Different for the
Better.

Isn't
That what Matters?

The Entry of the Gods into Valhalla, or the answer to a riddle

Whenever I
Listen to the
Piece, a part of a
Wagner opera, I
Imagine not only the
Arrivals of Norse warriors into the
Great
Hall, but the glorious
Deaths in
Combat that
Earned them each
Entrance to the
Place.

When I
Think of something to
Write about, I try to put the
Thought to
Paper immediately.
I do not want it to be
Lost. I do not want it to
Die. I do not want me to
Die.

I was in my car at the beach, on a
particularly
Beautiful
Day, the snow
Melting, birds
Chirping,
Clouds
Moving
Fast and
Low above the
Shore. I did not want to
Forget the moment. I felt
Compelled to
Write about it then.
But I didn't.

Yet I did not Forget about
It.

It was not just the
Clouds that had
Made the
Moment so
Beautiful.

Someone had told
me to not be
Mad at
Myself.
I didn't know that
I was, until they had
Suggested it.

It was True. And they made
me realize
That.

When I was
Driving away from the
Beach, I wanted to
Look back at the
Clouds. But
I did not, because
I knew that the only
Reason I
Yearned to
See them
Again was
Fear,
Fear that
I might lose the
Moment they
Represented.

Sometimes, I Think about a
girl I
like. she will Interrupt my
stream of thou

Driving away that day,
I actively decided to
Think about myself,
Instead.

Then, a bend in the
Road brought the
Sight of the
Clouds back to

Me.

12965315R00127

Made in the USA
Monee, IL
30 September 2019